ENGINEERING
DISASTERS

FORD PINTO FUEL TANKS

BY EMMA HUDDLESTON

CONTENT CONSULTANT
Patrick T. Hester, PhD, Associate Professor of Management,
Department of Management and Accountancy
University of North Carolina Asheville

Cover image: Ford Pinto models ran from 1971 to 1980.

Core Library
An Imprint of Abdo Publishing
abdobooks.com

abdobooks.com

Published by Abdo Publishing, a division of ABDO, PO Box 398166, Minneapolis, Minnesota 55439.

Printed in the United States of America, North Mankato, Minnesota
092019
012020

THIS BOOK CONTAINS RECYCLED MATERIALS

Cover Photo: AP Images
Interior Photos: AP Images, 1, 4–5, 29, 30, 34–35, 45; Keystone Pictures USA ZUMA Press/Newscom, 6; iStockphoto, 10; Marty Lederhandler/AP Images, 12–13; Bettmann/Getty Images, 14–15, 22; Shutterstock Images, 16 (top left), 16 (top right), 16 (bottom right); Jenson/Shutterstock Images, 16 (bottom left); Keystone-France/Gamma-Keystone/Getty Images, 19; JCH, File/AP Images, 24–25, 43; Jonathan Weiss/Shutterstock Images, 37; Salim Nasirov/Shutterstock Images, 40

Editor: Marie Pearson
Series Designer: Ryan Gale

Library of Congress Control Number: 2019942354

Publisher's Cataloging-in-Publication Data

Names: Huddleston, Emma, author.
Title: Ford Pinto fuel tanks / by Emma Huddleston
Description: Minneapolis, Minnesota : Abdo Publishing, 2020 | Series: Engineering disasters | Includes online resources and index.
Identifiers: ISBN 9781532190728 (lib. bdg.) | ISBN 9781532176579 (ebook)
Subjects: LCSH: Automobiles--Fuel tanks--Juvenile literature. | Ford automobiles--Juvenile literature. | Disasters--Juvenile literature. | Engineering--Juvenile literature. | Product recall--United States--Juvenile literature. | Explosions--Juvenile literature.
Classification: DDC 629.20--dc23

CONTENTS

CHAPTER ONE

UP IN FLAMES

In August 1978, three teenagers in Indiana got into their 1973 Ford Pinto to go to a volleyball game. Judy Ulrich drove. Her sister Donna and cousin Lyn were passengers. When they stopped to fill up on gas, they put the gas cap on top of the car. They forgot to put it back on. After a few miles on the highway, Judy noticed the cap fall off the car. She tried to pull over, but the highway had a curb. She couldn't get all the way off the road. She turned on her flashers

The Ulrichs were driving a 1973 Ford Pinto like this one when they were rear ended.

and slowed down. The driver behind her looked away for one moment. By the time he looked back, it was too late.

His van crashed into the Ulrichs' Pinto. The Pinto spun and slid 150 feet (45.7 m). Its gas tank burst and spilled gas. Then the car went up in flames. None of the Ulrich women survived the fire. Its temperature reached 1,300 degrees Fahrenheit (700°C). That was hot enough to melt the sunglasses Lyn wore. Lyn and Donna died right after the crash. Judy died eight hours later. She had burns on 95 percent of her body.

In the mid-1970s, stories about Pintos catching fire started to spread in the United States. News reports and court cases reported it happening after rear-end collisions. But the Ulrichs were not aware of the danger. Their family didn't get a recall notice until a few months after the accident.

The Pinto's popularity was helped by available features such as a sunroof.

PERSPECTIVES

PINTO WAS POPULAR

At first, the Pinto was popular. Its first year was 1971. Sales in California were high despite the fact that imported cars were especially popular there. Reviews of the Pinto were better than expected. People thought the engine worked well, and the large doors made it easy to get in and out. Ford sold 328,275 Pintos in the first year. The highest selling year for the Pinto was 1973 with 479,668 sold. Ford also had a strong reputation in the car industry. The Pinto and Mercury Bobcat became top-selling subcompacts in America. The Mercury Bobcat was a similar model.

WHEN AND WHY WAS THE PINTO MADE?

Ford Motor Company made the Pinto. Ford has been one of the leading manufacturers in the US car industry since the early 1900s. It first sold the Model T in 1908. This vehicle was affordable and reliable. By 1918, almost half the cars in the United States were Model Ts. Over the years, the company continued to be successful. But it had tough competition from companies around the world.

Foreign competition sparked the creation of the Pinto. Sales for imported cars were rising in the 1960s. The Volkswagen Beetle and Toyota Corolla were popular models. They were subcompact cars. Subcompacts were the smallest class of cars. They were smaller, lighter, and cheaper than other models. If Ford wanted more people to buy its cars, it had to lower its prices. This meant making its own subcompact. So it

OTHER DANGEROUS SUBCOMPACTS

Car safety expert Byron Bloch found the Pinto was not the only dangerous subcompact of its time. It was similar in size and shape to other subcompact models. Some had thin gas tank metal. Others had weak bumpers. In 1975 and 1976, hundreds of crashes involving subcompacts ended with one or more deaths. The Pinto ranked in the middle of a group of seven models. The model with the most deaths was Datsun 1200/210. In 1976, 418 people died in Datsun crashes.

Despite their history, Pintos are popular collector cars today.

created the Pinto. The Pinto had a long front and short back end. It came in bold colors including red, yellow, and green.

INVESTIGATING THE DISASTER

The Ulrichs' Pinto explosion led to the 1979 court case *State of Indiana v. Ford Motor Company*. This was the first time a US corporation was charged with murder. It was also the first time a US company was taken to court for dangerous product design. Ford was found not guilty. Ford explained that the Pinto fuel tank design was similar to that of other subcompacts. Additionally, Ford followed all the rules for safety recalls. It sent letters out as quickly as possible, and it offered repairs. Ford won the case. But other investigations showed the company was not completely innocent. The company knew the Pinto could have been made safer.

EXPLORE ONLINE

Chapter One talks about Ford Motor Company and its role in making cars. Explore this website about how cars are made. Compare and contrast the website with this chapter. What new information did you learn?

WONDEROPOLIS: HOW ARE CARS MADE?

abdocorelibrary.com/ford-pinto-fuel-tanks

CHAPTER TWO

DESIGN AND SAFETY

Lee Iacocca was an executive vice president at Ford. When the company was brainstorming how to compete with foreign models, Iacocca suggested the Pinto. He focused on making it low cost and lightweight. His idea helped get him promoted to president of Ford in 1970.

Iacocca's plans for the weight and price were known as the limits of 2,000. The car could not weigh more than 2,000 pounds (907 kg). It could not sell for more than $2,000. Both limits helped make the car affordable.

Lee Iacocca wanted to create a car that would compete with overseas companies. The Pinto program started in August 1968.

The Ford Pinto was one of the top-selling subcompact cars in the United States at the time.

And over time, people would spend less money on gas to fuel it. Lighter cars don't need as much gas to move.

RUSHED BUILD TIME

Ford rushed to design and build the Pinto. It wanted to sell the car as soon as possible. It worked on the

Pinto for 25 months. The normal amount of time was 43 months. The rush was a risk. Ford didn't give engineers enough time to work out some defects.

The Pinto had several defects. The tube for filling up the gas tank was not very secure. It could easily

MAKING A VEHICLE

This diagram shows the usual process of making a new model of vehicle. How does it help you understand what steps would have been affected and why it would have been so expensive to change the Ford Pinto's fuel tank when the issue was noticed?

1. Designing the Vehicle

2. Tooling (Designing the Tools to Make the Vehicle)

3. Assembling the Vehicle

4. Selling the Vehicle

break from the tank in a crash and spray gas. The wheel well panel could separate from the floor of the car in a crash too. This added to the danger of the defective tube. More gas could leak into the cabin. Metal car parts could scrape on the ground and spark a fire. Four sharp bolts pointed at the gas tank. Nothing covered them, so they could easily puncture the tank in a crash and spill gas.

Some of these defects were discovered in the design process. But because of the rushed timeline, design and tooling overlapped. Tooling was the part of the production process when the machines to build the Pinto were made. Since the machines were already tooled, fixing the defects would be expensive. Some Ford engineers knew the Pinto had faults. But the company had no time or money to fix them. Iacocca's limits left no extra money to spend on protecting the fuel system.

RISKY DESIGN

Iacocca's plans were great for selling the car. But they didn't focus on safety. At that time, the whole car industry did not prioritize safety. The idea "safety doesn't sell" came from an unsuccessful Ford campaign in 1956. Ford tried selling cars by telling people how safe they were. Still, their sales dropped. It seemed people were not interested in safety features. They cared more about style and price.

For this reason, protecting the gas tank was not a priority in the Pinto. It was located between the rear axle and the bumper. The main reason it was put there was because it allowed for more trunk space. Most subcompacts didn't have large trunks, so this made the Pinto stand out compared to other models.

However, this location only left 9 inches (23 cm) of crush space. Crush space protects the gas tank during an accident. It is extra room for the metal of the car to fold or bend in before hitting the gas tank.

To fix fuel tank issues, Ford would have needed to pay more than $110 million. The company decided that cost was too high and proceeded with production.

Additionally, the tank hung down below the bumper. Objects could easily hit it from behind. The bumper was not very strong. It was for looks more than safety.

There were three ways Ford could have protected the fuel system. All options cost less than $9 per car, but none were used. They were thrown out as extra cost and weight due to Iacocca's limits of 2,000.

MOTOR VEHICLE SAFETY ACT OF 1966

The Motor Vehicle Safety Act of 1966 was the first federal law about car safety. Manufacturers would then be responsible for safety issues when their products were used. Previously, cars were not expected to survive accidents. Many accidents were linked to driver errors or bad roads. Car companies claimed that cars were as safe as possible when used normally. But there was no definition of normal. Car companies did not feel responsible for making cars with strong crash protection. Accidents were not considered normal use.

SAFETY STANDARDS

The Pinto was designed in the late 1960s. The first vehicle safety laws were created at the same time. This was a sign that people were starting to care about safety.

Ford built the Pinto as more federal regulations were becoming law. In particular, the National Highway and Traffic Safety Administration (NHTSA) Standard 301 affected the Pinto. It was about fuel system design and safety. The NHTSA was created in 1970 as the

National Highway Safety Bureau. It carries out safety programs. It educates people about safety tips. It sets safety standards for car and truck design. Its purpose is to make driving safer.

The first version of Standard 301 from 1967 only covered front-end crashes. In 1969, NHTSA (at that time the National Highway Safety Bureau) included rear-end crashes. Ford approved the standard and tested multiple cars. In the test, a 4,000-pound (1,814-kg) flat barrier was moved at 20 mph (32 km/h) until it hit the back of a nonmoving car. The car had to

PERSPECTIVES

FORD FIGHTS REGULATIONS

Some people in the car industry resisted change. Regulations limited how cars could be made. Ford had multiple leaders who fought regulations. Henry Ford II was the head of Ford in the late 1900s. Part of the reason he fought safety regulations was to protect the company's profit. The more regulations a company has to meet, the more money it spends to make the car. The company then has to sell the car for more money.

The 1971 Pinto was not required to meet the newest NHTSA regulations.

survive the hit, and the gas tank could not burst. Based on the test, Ford made slight changes to the Pinto's design. None had been manufactured yet.

Then in 1970, a few days after the first Pintos sold, NHTSA suggested a stricter regulation. It wanted Standard 301 to include a fixed-barrier test. The test required the car to move and hit a still barrier. This type of crash was more severe. NHTSA also wanted to change the speed of the car from 20 miles per hour (32 km/h) to 30 miles per hour (48 km/h). It was much more difficult to design a car that would not roll over or burst into flames in these conditions. But the regulation would not affect the 1971 to 1976 Pintos. It only applied to 1977 cars and later.

In 1970, Ford thought it was fair to expect the fuel tank to survive this type of test. It made slight changes to the 1973 Pinto model. But it did not agree that a car should be able to resist rolling over in this type of accident. It wrote a report to NHTSA explaining why it didn't think the regulation should be approved. Eventually, that report would lead to accusations against Ford.

FURTHER EVIDENCE

Chapter Two explains safety standards at the time the Pinto was created. What is one of the main points of this chapter? What evidence does the author use to support this point? The website below has information about the history of NHTSA. Find a quote from the website that supports the chapter's main point.

UNDERSTANDING THE NATIONAL HIGHWAY TRAFFIC SAFETY ADMINISTRATION (NHTSA)

abdocorelibrary.com/ford-pinto-fuel-tanks

CHAPTER THREE

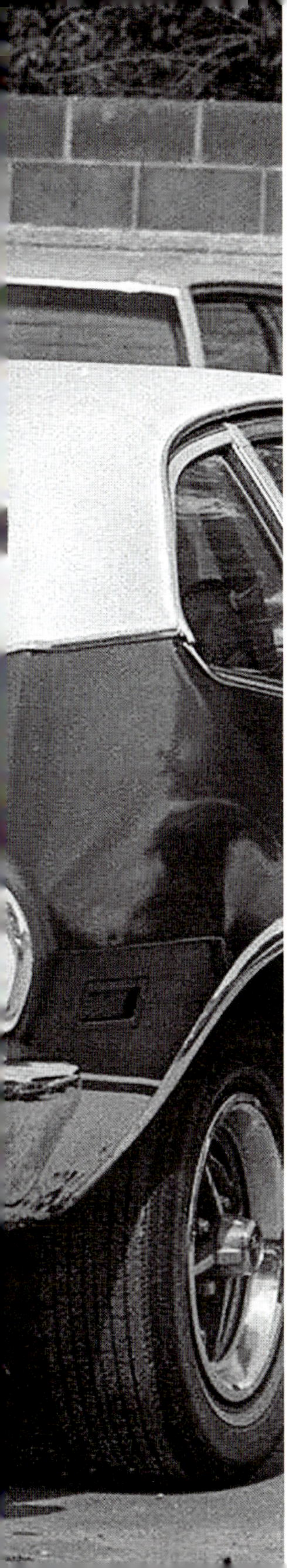

INVESTIGATIONS

In the mid-1970s, several Pintos burst into flames in rear-end crashes. This led Mark Dowie, a writer for *Mother Jones* magazine, to investigate Ford and the Pinto. Dowie published an article titled "Pinto Madness" in 1977. Dowie emphasized the fact that Ford chose not to use a $1 rubber piece to protect the gas tank from the four sharp bolts near it.

In 1991, law professor Gary T. Schwartz published a report about the article. He noted it contained exaggerations and even false facts. Dowie's article inspired more fear than was necessary. It misrepresented Ford's report to the NHTSA. It made it seem as

One Pinto owner sent a message to other drivers in 1978 by displaying a warning sign on her 1975 Ford Pinto.

though Ford carelessly sold Pintos with defects because the company only wanted money. One false fact estimated that 500 to 900 people burned to death because of design flaws. In reality, fewer than 30 people had died because of rear-end crash fires. Still, the *Mother Jones* article led to more investigations. People wanted to know whether Ford knew of the dangers. Some people wondered why Ford didn't use a safer

PERSPECTIVES

BLAMING FORD, SCARING PEOPLE

Los Angeles, California, auto safety expert Byron Bloch did an in-depth study of the Pinto fuel system. His findings were part of the *Mother Jones* article. He said, "It's a catastrophic blunder. Ford made an extremely irresponsible decision when they placed such a weak tank in such a ridiculous location in such a soft rear end. It's almost designed to blow up." But researchers have noted that the Pinto was just as safe as other subcompact cars. In 1975 and 1976, it had caused fewer deaths than either the Beetle or the Corolla.

saddle-type tank design. This design put the tank above the wheels and trunk.

CONTROVERSIAL REPORT

People questioned Ford's report to the NHTSA in 1973 about Standard 301. They thought it was evidence that Ford was trying to hide the Pinto's defects. But the report was about the rollover standard, not the rear-end crash suggestions. It did include a cost-benefit analysis that put a price on human life. Ford used an estimated $200,000 for the cost of a life and $67,000 for the cost of a person's injuries after

SADDLE-TYPE TANK DESIGN

The saddle-type tank design locates the gas tank over the rear axle. It is a safer design, but it limits trunk space. Some other Ford models used this safer design. Ford owned the patent to it. The Pinto was not the only car that didn't use the saddle-type tank. Other subcompacts had risky fuel tank systems too. The Pinto's system was just studied more closely than others because of the accidents that went to court.

a crash. Then it used the numbers to calculate whether spending $11 per car on safety pieces was worth it. The report said added safety would have avoided 180 deaths and 180 serious burn injuries. The death and injuries would cost $49.5 million. On the other hand, the cost of making 12.5 million vehicles safer was $137 million.

Two things are significant about these numbers. First, Ford did not come up with the cost of human life. The NHTSA determined that price in 1972. Ford was simply using the NHTSA's numbers. In addition, when Ford considered the cost of making 12.5 million cars, it was referring to all cars made in the United States, not just its own. This led experts to later explain that Ford wasn't fighting for its own budget. It was fighting for the whole US car industry. All car manufacturers at the time thought the fixed-barrier test was too strict. But Ford's analysis was flawed. Later investigations suggested that

In the 1980 *State of Indiana v. Ford Motor Company* trial, evidence included a photo of a test crash done by Ford, *top*, and a photo of the Ulrichs' Pinto after their crash, *bottom*.

#17
4382 I
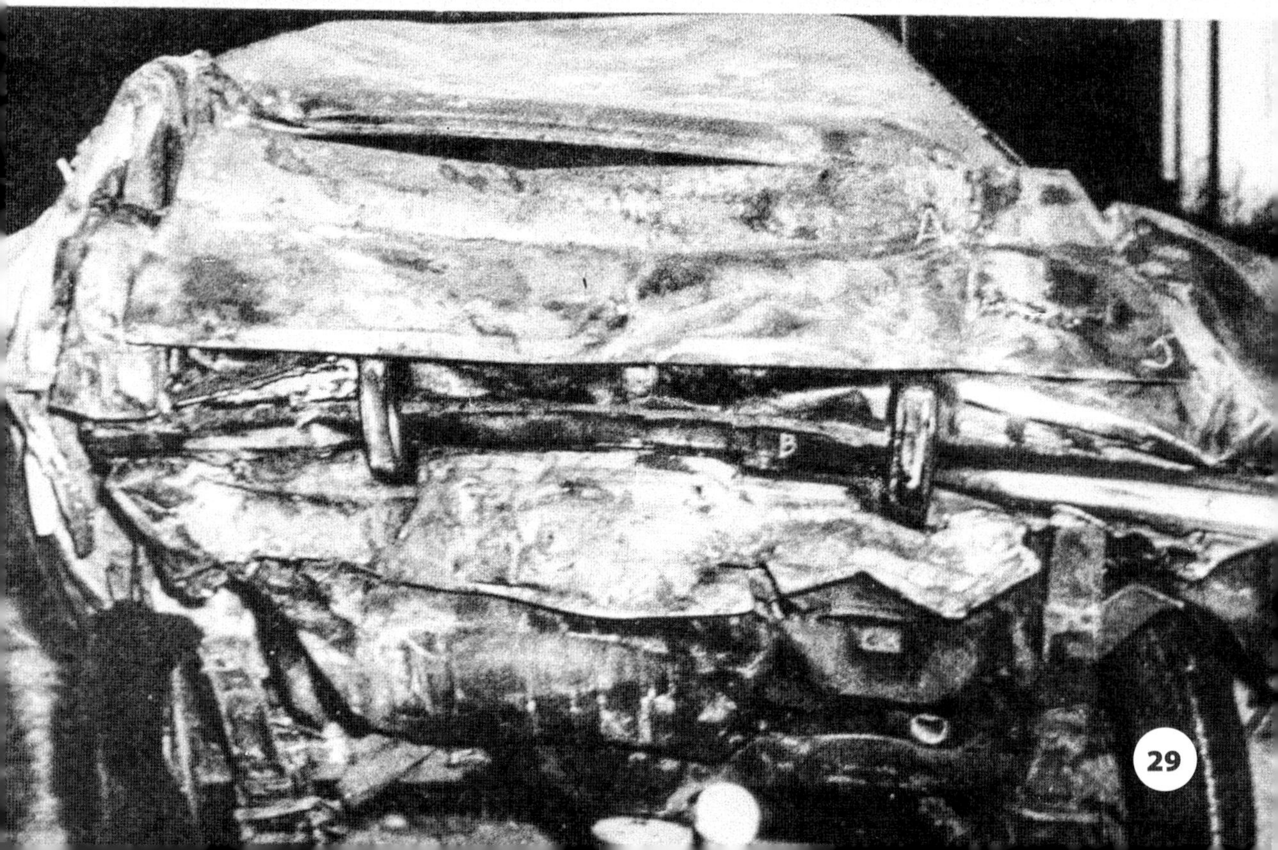

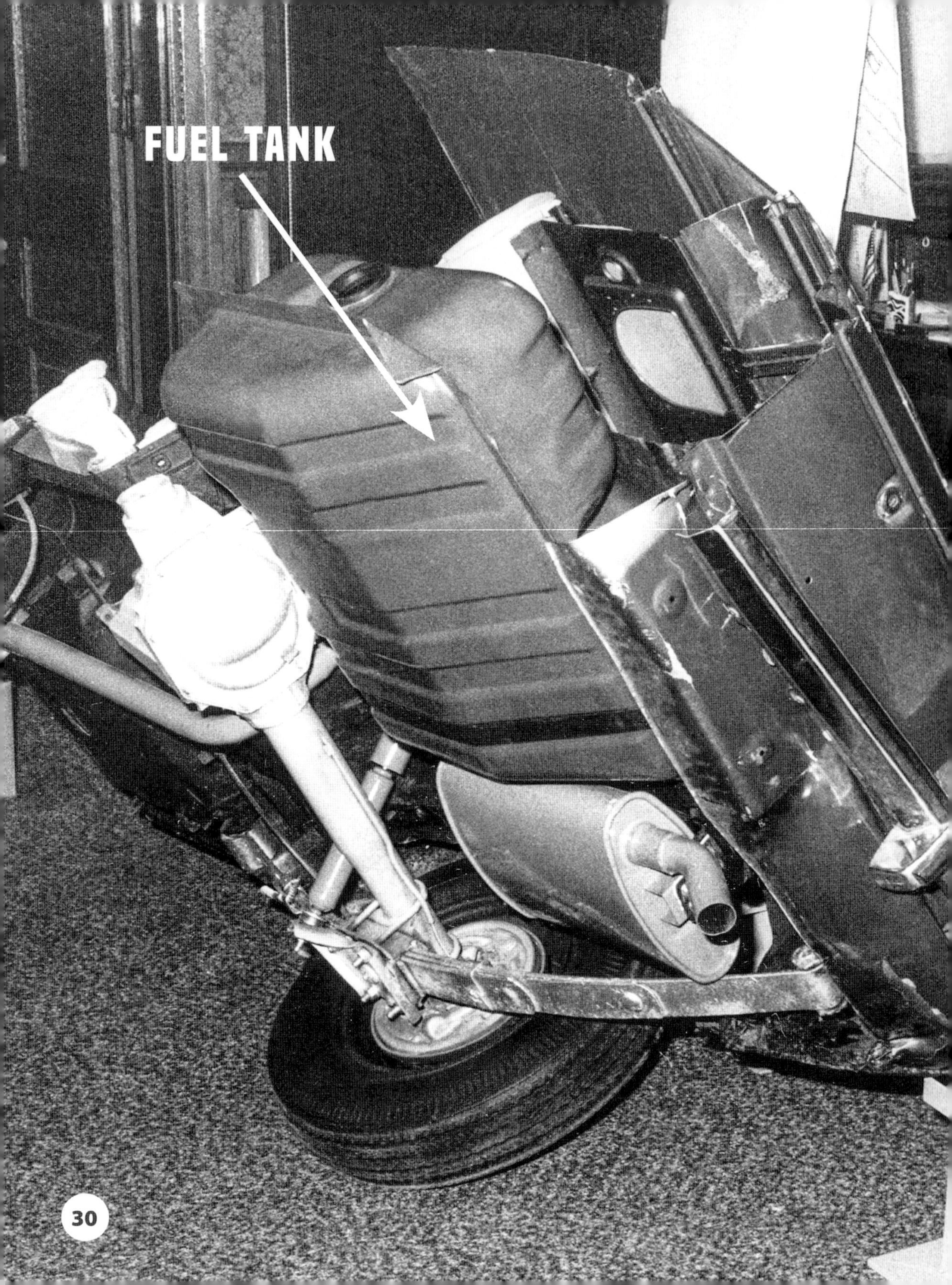
FUEL TANK

safety pieces only cost $5 or $9 per car. Both options are cheaper than Ford's estimate of $11, though these fixes would still have cost more than Ford's estimate of cost of death and injuries.

ONE OF MANY LAWSUITS

Still, there was an issue with the Pinto's design. Pinto fuel tank fires led to 117 lawsuits. Ford faced lots of criticism. Some was a result of the *Mother Jones* article and misunderstandings about the report.

One case was *Grimshaw v. Ford*. The accident happened in May 1972. The court case ended in February 1978. In 1972, Lilly Gray was driving 13-year-old Richard Grimshaw home. They were neighbors. They were suddenly hit from behind. The car that crashed into them was going approximately 35 miles per hour (56 km/h). The fuel tank of Gray's car was punctured in the crash. Gas spilled and caught

A cutaway of the back of the Pinto shows how close the fuel tank was to the car's bumper.

on fire. Some leaked into Grimshaw's seat. He was burned on 95 percent of his body. He had more than 52 surgeries after the accident. Gray died.

One of the most shocking discoveries during the investigation proved that Ford engineers knew of the fuel tank defects. But the company chose not to protect the tank.

Grimshaw was awarded $6 million. Gray's family got almost $560,000 for her wrongful death. The ruling set a standard for the ethics of car manufacturers. Companies would be punished if they put people's lives at risk to save money.

STRAIGHT TO THE SOURCE

In Mark Dowie's *Mother Jones* article, Dowie interviewed a Ford engineer. The engineer said:

> *This company is run by salesmen, not engineers; so the priority is styling, not safety. . . . There are a few of us here at Ford who are concerned about fire safety. . . . But we don't talk about it much. It isn't a popular subject. I've never seen safety on the agenda of a product meeting and, except for a brief period in 1956, I can't remember seeing the word safety in an advertisement. I really don't think the company wants American consumers to start thinking too much about safety—for fear they might demand it, I suppose.*

Source: Mark Dowie. "Pinto Madness." *Mother Jones*. Mother Jones, September/October 1977. Web. Accessed May 9, 2019.

What's the Big Idea?

Read the primary source text carefully and determine its main idea. Explain how the main idea is supported by details, naming two or three of those supporting details. It is important to know that the *Mother Jones* article is not necessarily reliable for facts. However, it still brings up important ethical issues. Do you think Ford was wrong for how it made and sold Pintos? Why or why not?

CHAPTER FOUR

PINTOS RECALLED

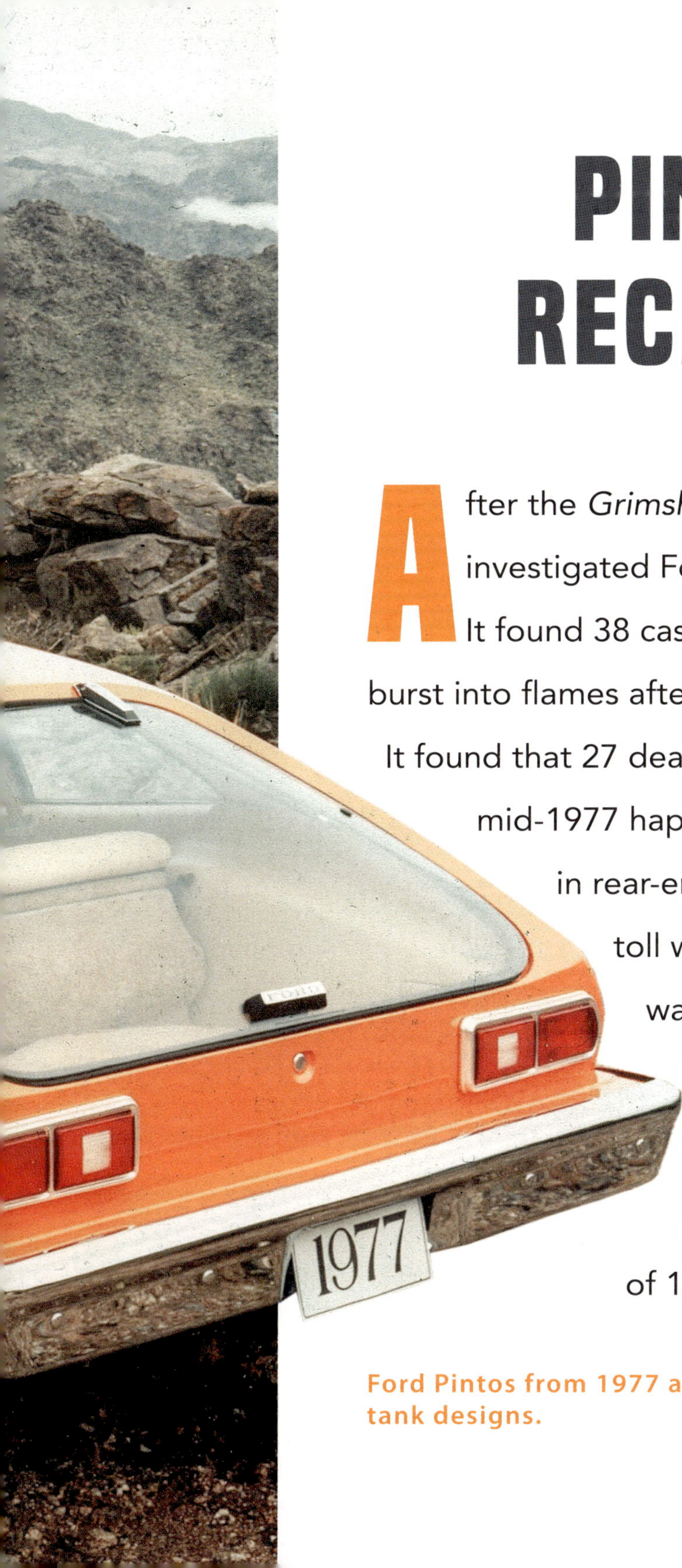

After the *Grimshaw v. Ford* case, NHTSA investigated Ford and the Pinto. It found 38 cases in which the Pinto burst into flames after a rear-end crash. It found that 27 deaths between 1970 and mid-1977 happened because of fires in rear-end crashes. The death toll was significant, but it was not as dramatic as Dowie's estimates.

Ford chose to recall some Pintos in the fall of 1978 after the NHTSA

Ford Pintos from 1977 and later had improved fuel tank designs.

investigation and *Mother Jones* article. The recall affected 1.5 million Pintos sold from 1971 to 1976. It also included 30,000 Mercury Bobcats that had the same fuel tank design. Not only was the reputation of the Pinto ruined, but Ford needed to change the fuel tank defects. The car had to pass the stricter Standard 301 test. Six people died during the time that Ford decided to do a recall and safer parts were available to fix their cars. Three of the people who died were the Ulrich women.

The fuel system was made safer by changing the tube that connected to the gas tank. It was longer and had a better clamp to secure it to the tank. A plastic shield was added to the fuel tank too. This protected it from sharp bolts. Pinto models from 1977 on had this safer design. But the damage to the Pinto's reputation had been done. The last year Ford sold the Pinto was 1980.

Ford continues to be a popular automaker.

MESSAGE TO THE CAR INDUSTRY

The message to the car industry was that safety is important. Ford was extremely focused on the cost of building and selling the Pinto. It ended up paying millions in damages and millions more lobbying against safety standards. Its cost-benefit analysis showed it would be cheaper to pay for accidents and lawsuits than to pay to make Pintos safer. But Ford ended up spending much more than it predicted. Making, selling, recalling, and fixing Pintos cost the company more than doing it right the first time.

The drama and investigation of Ford Pintos ended the idea that "safety doesn't sell." Many car companies began emphasizing safety features afterward. This can be seen in commercials and advertisements today. For example, a 2019 Nissan Altima commercial tagline was "surround yourself with safety."

PERSPECTIVES

PINTO LOVERS

Norm Bagi owns a light blue 1977 Pinto. He is one of many people who drives in the Pinto Stampede event in Michigan. Bagi said, "The Ford Pinto was an indisputable sales success whose safety record turned out to be as good as or better than its competitors. Despite the fire myth that will forever follow this little car into eternity, it's still gratifying to see so many people smile and give a 'thumbs-up' when they see our Pintos driving down the road together. We're all still very proud of our Pintos!" Despite their safety issues, many people still love the Ford Pinto as a collector's item.

CAR SAFETY TODAY

Ethics and product liability are important issues for people today. Product liability court cases, like the Pinto cases, determine whether or not a company is responsible for accidents that happen when people use its products. These cases often lead to stronger safety standards.

For example, SUVs in the 2000s were dangerous because they rolled over easily. Thousands of people died. Then, federal regulations forced car companies to change SUV designs. Old SUVs were tall and narrow. They easily rolled over on tight curves or sudden swerves. New SUVs were made with a wider wheel base. This made them more stable.

The Ford Pinto fuel tank disaster

SAFE TECHNOLOGY

Technology is a big part of car safety today. Engineers are working to make voice control systems better. This could let drivers control the temperature, music, and lights by talking. They would not have to take their hands off the wheel or eyes off the road. Additionally, many cars have rearview cameras that help drivers see what is behind the car. This is helpful for driving in reverse.

COMPARING FUEL TANKS

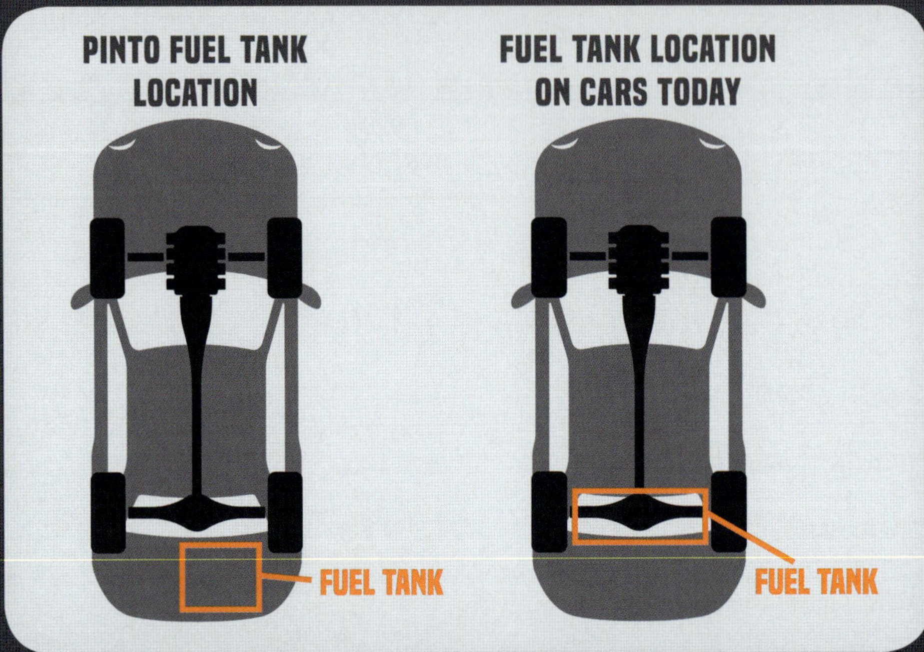

This diagram shows the location of the fuel tank in the Pinto compared to its common location in cars today. How does today's location keep the tank safer?

was a result of many risky but legal decisions. Federal regulations did not force Ford to focus on safety at the time. Today, standards require that car companies make cars as safe as possible.

STRAIGHT TO THE SOURCE

Denny Gioia worked in the recall office at Ford in the early 1970s. He traced common problems until enough information built up a case. He said of the work:

> *[Ford] had identified twelve highway tractors, the big ones, where they knew the front hubs were going to break. . . . And so we dropped everything. . . . We stayed up for several days until we found them all. One was in Alaska. Another was on a boat to Hawaii.*
>
> *So many people . . . are saying, "It's a collection of bad actors, and they have [become hardened] to their responsibilities." But I think it's important to say that, at least in the recall office where I worked, it was not populated by a collection of ogres. They were people that cared.*

Source: Malcolm Gladwell. "The Engineer's Lament." *The New Yorker*. Condé Nast, April 27, 2015. Web. Accessed May 9, 2019.

Point of View

Read both primary source texts in the book and think about the two writers' points of view. Write a short essay that answers: What is the point of view of each author? How are they similar and why? How are they different and why?

FAST FACTS

- Ford Motor Company made Pintos in the 1970s to compete with foreign imports. The Pinto was a subcompact car.
- Lee Iacocca came up with the idea for the Pinto and made the limits of 2,000. The Pinto was meant to sell for $2,000 and weigh no more than 2,000 pounds (907 kg).
- The Pinto design put the gas tank in a risky location. It also had defects including the tube that connected to the gas tank. It could easily separate from the tank and spill gas.
- Engineers at Ford knew the Pinto had defects. However, the rushed build time and Iacocca's limits led to Ford's decision to make and sell the Pinto anyway.
- In a controversial report to the NHTSA, Ford compared the costs of paying for people's injuries to the costs of making all cars made in America safer. The report concluded that it was cheaper to pay for potential injuries, put people's lives at risk, and leave cars as they were.
- Pintos were involved in many rear-end crashes. In 38 cases, the fuel tank burst and caught fire. A NHTSA investigation found that 27 people died from fires in rear-end crashes from 1970 to mid-1977.

- Ford chose to recall the 1971–1976 models after the NHTSA investigation. Federal regulations added gas tank protection and made changes to the defective tube for 1977 and later models.
- The Pinto disasters and their court cases sent a message to the car industry that safety mattered. Today, many car companies focus on a variety of safety features.

STOP AND THINK

Tell the Tale

Chapters One and Three of this book discuss important Pinto disasters. Imagine you are a news reporter. Write 200 words about these disasters. How would you describe Ford and the Pinto while relying on facts?

Surprise Me

Chapter Two discusses some of the defects in the Pinto. After reading this book, what two or three facts about the Pinto design did you find most surprising? Write a few sentences about each fact. Why did you find each fact surprising?

Dig Deeper

After reading this book, what questions do you still have about the Ford Pinto? With an adult's help, find a few reliable sources that can help you answer your questions. Write a paragraph about what you learned.

Say What?

Studying how cars are made can mean learning a lot of new vocabulary. Find five words in this book you've never heard before. Use a dictionary to find out what they mean. Then write the meanings in your own words, and use each word in a new sentence.

GLOSSARY

axle
a rod in a car where wheels attach to each end

cabin
the open area inside a car where people sit

cost-benefit analysis
a type of test that weighs the costs of two options to decide which one will most benefit the company or make the company more money

defect
a problem or part made incorrectly

ethics
moral issues or values

imported
coming from another country

lobbying
trying to convince government officials to make a certain decision

patent
a document that shows ownership of an invention

recall
to call back products because they are dangerous or need to be changed

regulation
a rule made by an organization or the government

tooling
to build the machines that will make a product

ONLINE RESOURCES

To learn more about Ford Pinto fuel tanks, visit our free resource websites below.

Core Library CONNECTION
FREE! COMMON CORE MULTIMEDIA RESOURCES

Visit **abdocorelibrary.com** or scan this QR code for free Common Core resources for teachers and students, including vetted activities, multimedia, and booklinks, for deeper subject comprehension.

Booklinks NONFICTION NETWORK
FREE! ONLINE NONFICTION RESOURCES

Visit **abdobooklinks.com** or scan this QR code for free additional online weblinks for further learning. These links are routinely monitored and updated to provide the most current information available.

LEARN MORE

Doudna, Kelly. *Automobiles: From Henry Ford to Elon Musk.* Minneapolis, MN: Abdo Publishing, 2019.

Dutta, Suneha. *Cars: Facts at Your Fingertips.* New York: DK Publishing, 2016.

INDEX

About the Author

Emma Huddleston lives in the Twin Cities with her husband. She enjoys writing educational books, but she likes reading novels even more. When she is not writing or reading, she likes to stay active by running and swing dancing.